This book belongs to

_____

Loyola Press

3441 North Ashland Avenue
Chicago, Illinois 60657

Interior design by Amy Olson

Library of Congress Cataloging-in-Publication Data

Walsh, Mary Caswell.
    Saint Francis celebrates Christmas / retold by Mary Caswell Walsh;
illustrated by Helen Caswell.
        p.   cm.
    "A true story based on Thomas of Celano's thirteenth-century
biography of Saint Francis of Assisi."
    Summary: Recounts St. Francis of Assisi's reenactment of the
manger scene of the birth of Jesus, and how that led to the use of
small nativity scenes in people's homes at Christmas.
    ISBN 0-8294-1112-7
    1. Francis, of Assisi, Saint, 1182–1226.   2. Christian saints—
Italy—Assisi—Biography—Juvenile literature.   3. Crèches
(Nativity scenes)—Juvenile literature.   4. Christmas—Juvenile
literature.   [1. Francis, of Assisi, Saint, 1182–1226.   2. Crèches
(Nativity scenes)   3. Christmas.]   I. Thomas, of Celano, fl.1257.
II. Caswell, Helen Rayburn, ill.   III. Title.
BX4700.F69W35 1998
271'.302
[B]—DC21

                           98-6536
                           CIP
                           AC

Printed in the United States of America
98 99 00 01 02 / 10 9 8 7 6 5 4 3 2 1

Saint Francis Celebrates
CHRISTMAS

A true story based on Thomas of Celano's thirteenth-century
biography of Saint Francis of Assisi

Retold by Mary Caswell Walsh
Illustrated by Helen Caswell

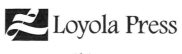 Loyola Press

Chicago

Saint Francis loved Christmas.

One year while
he was staying
near the little town of Gréccio, Francis had an
idea for a special way to celebrate Christmas.
The more he thought about it, the more he liked
his idea.

He asked his friend John to help him. John was a
good man, and Francis loved him.

"If you want to celebrate Christmas with me," Francis told John, "go quickly and bring me a wooden box."

"A wooden box?" asked John.

"Big enough to hold a chicken," said Francis.

"Now what does he want with a box?" John wondered, but he went and did as Francis had asked.

He found the carpenter in his workshop. The carpenter had a box that was just the right size, and he let John borrow it.

John brought the box to Francis, and Francis was pleased.

"Now I need some hay," said Francis.

"Hay?" John asked.

"A bushel," said Francis.

"What can he possibly want with a bushel of hay?" John said to himself, but he did as Francis wanted. John went to his friend the farmer and asked him for a bushel of hay.

When John brought the hay to Francis, Francis was pleased.

"Now I need an ox," he said.

"An ox?" John asked.

"And a donkey," said Francis.

"What is he going to do with an ox and a donkey?" John wondered, but he did as his friend had asked. He went back to the farmer, who was happy to let him borrow the animals. John led the ox, but the farmer's son had to help with the donkey.

Francis was happy to see John and the farmer's son with the ox and donkey.

"Now I need three tall men," he said.

"Three men?" John asked.

"Wearing purple," said Francis.

"Why purple?" John said to himself, but he went and asked the banker, the storekeeper, and the doctor to come. The banker wore his purple vest, the storekeeper wore his daughter's scarf, and the doctor wore a tunic made out of an old purple tablecloth.

When Francis saw that John had brought the three men, he was pleased.

"Now I need some sheep," he said.

"Sheep?" asked John.

"Yes, sheep," said Francis. "I think three will be enough."

"I can't imagine what he wants with sheep," John thought, but he went to do as Francis had asked. At John's request, the shepherd brought three of his sheep, a dog, and a cat.

By this time everyone in Gréccio had heard that Francis was up to something. Many of the children came running and crowding around Francis. "We want to come too!" they cried.

"Of course you may come," Francis said. "It wouldn't be Christmas without you. Go home

and tell your parents to bring candles and torches and meet us in the clearing beside the woods."

So the children hurried home to fetch their parents.

Then Francis said to John, "Now I need a baby."

"A baby?" John asked.

"And the baby's mother, of course."

"Of course," said John, shaking his head.

"Why on earth does he need a baby?" John said to himself, but he went home to see his wife.

"Francis needs you and our baby to come to his Christmas celebration," he told her.

"What fun!" she cried as she wrapped the baby in a soft blanket and went with John to see what Francis would do next.

Francis was glad to see them.

"Quickly," he said to all he had gathered, "before the others arrive with their candles and torches, let me tell you what we will do."

He told them what he had in mind, and everyone did as he asked.

Even the donkey.

At last it was Christmas Eve. The first stars shone in the sky, and on the earth the fireflies flickered.

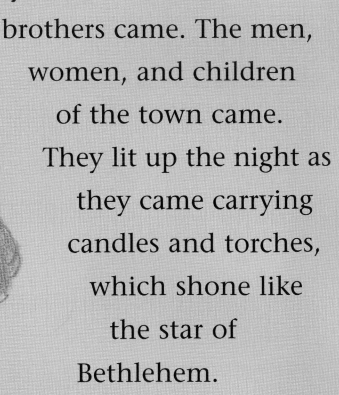

Then they came. Francis's brothers came. The men, women, and children of the town came. They lit up the night as they came carrying candles and torches, which shone like the star of Bethlehem.

Francis stood before the manger, sighing.
He was overcome with love and filled with a
wonderful happiness.

The people looked upon the manger and were filled with new joy as they celebrated the miracle of Christ's birth.

That night has not been forgotten.

In homes throughout the world, families still set out the manger scene and gaze with love and wonder on the ox, the shepherd and his sheep, the three kings, Joseph, Mary, and the dear Christ Child.

And, yes, even the donkey.